MILLIPEDE
AND
COCKROACH

CONTENTS

Front cover painting by:
D A Lish

Photos by:
Nick Baker

©1999 by Kingdom Books PO9 5TL ENGLAND

INTRODUCTION

When you decide to keep cockroaches or millipedes, you will be quizzed and questioned ruthlessly by friends and relatives as to 'why keep those revolting creatures?' and you will undoubtedly hear phrases such as 'you should have stuck to hamsters'. But move beyond the bad image of these beasts and you will discover a small world with a big fascination.

It may seem strange to include cockroaches and millipedes in the same book: they look different, have different life cycles, move in different ways and have different numbers of legs and body segments. Therefore it comes as no surprise to find that they are very different kinds of creatures, not even closely related. Cockroaches are insects whilst millipedes belong to a group of animals called Myriapods (mir-e-ah-pods) which means 'many legs' and includes both the centipedes and the millipedes.

Putting them in the same book is very practical in that many species of both types of animal require similar living and breeding conditions. They are both mainly opportunist *detritivores*, scraping out an existence among the leaf litter and soil, eating just about any decaying vegetable matter from fruit to dead wood, scavenging for this in the darkest and dankest of places.

What's The Appeal?

It is fair to say that you cannot love your pet cockroach or millipede in the same way that you can a cat or a dog. They cannot cuddle up to you on the sofa, they will not fetch your slippers and, if you call them, they won't come scuttling. It would seem that fluffy creatures have the monopoly in the popularity stakes.

Invertebrate pets have a different kind of attraction, with an appeal similar to that of fish and turtles. They are creatures that we like to observe, to sit in front of and ponder, to contemplate their ways, which are so far removed from our own or our domestic breeds. They have many advantages too. They do not need regular exercise, they are easy to feed, they do not wake the neighbours with their howling, nor do they leave hairs on your clothes or sofa. Above all, they do not require much space so it is easy to recreate suitable conditions for them in just about any home.

By the time you have finished this book, hopefully you will have enough background knowledge about the life history, behaviour and husbandry of cockroaches and millipedes to be able to keep, breed and get the most out of your new-found, fascinating and somewhat alternative pets.

What Is A Millipede?

Translated, the word 'millipede' means 1000 feet! This is rather ambitious as even the beast holding the 'most legs award' has got only 375 pairs, making a total of 750. Most have far fewer – in the region of 200–300 when they are adult.

A handful of millipedes.

They are often confused with the predatory centipedes which superficially resemble millipedes; though they are not strictly related, scientists lump them together in the group Myriapoda. The two species can easily be distinguished in that centipedes have only one pair of legs per segment whilst millipedes have two.

Millipedes have been around for over 400 million years. Fossil remains of ancient creatures of similar type suggest that they may have grown to over 1.5 metres (5ft) long, making them the largest invertebrates (creatures without backbones) ever to have walked on land!

Today there are over 10,000 different recorded kinds from around the world and they come in a dazzling variety of sizes and shapes from the tiny, about 2mm (0.10in) long, to the giants, which can reach nearly 30cm (12in) in length. There are rounded ones that look for all the world like Hoover tubes with legs, flattened plated ones and short dumpy ones that can curl up into a ball.

By simply looking around your garden or the local park, among the dead leaves under the hedge, in the rockery and under bark, you can often find a variety of native millipedes that fit nearly all these descriptions and a great deal can be learnt from them. However, as the largest of these only reaches about 3.5cm (just over an inch), details of their lives will be revealed only with the help of a magnifying lens.

Many of the more spectacular and exotic forms of millipede can now be obtained easily from breeders and some of the specialised pet shops. Despite living and behaving in much the same way as their smaller native cousins, their sheer size and range of colours make them appealing pets.

What Is A Cockroach?

Apart from being probably the most despised and detested creature on the planet, the cockroach is also one of the most successful. It has been around for something like 340 million years and in that time it has managed to conquer many different habitats from forests, deserts and mountains to behind the kitchen cabinet!

Most cockroach species are found in and around the tropics. It is only when certain species become associated with humans and hitch rides all around the globe that they become cockroaches out of their proper environment and this is when you get the 'pest' cockroach.

Today there are over 4000 described species of cockroach and, out of these, only 25 (less than 1%) are really serious pests, tarnishing the name of the rest of this group of fascinating insects.

Many of these are small, fast scuttlers and this quality alone makes them unsuitable as everyday pets. However, there are a few large and relatively sluggish species that are very easy to keep as pets and are a good introduction to the lives and ways of insects in general. See the chapter on Choosing on page 17.

HOUSING

Housing your cockroach or millipede is not difficult. They have few needs, but it is important to remember what those needs are.

The Vivarium

The word 'vivarium' sounds technical, but simply means a cage that can be set up to house creatures in conditions as near their wild settings as possible. In the case of millipedes and cockroaches this is a very simple task, as most are happy in just about any form of housing that contains soil, shelter, moisture and food.

The vivarium should be twice as long and twice as wide as its longest inhabitant.

To some extent, what kind of housing you wish to give your millipedes or cockroaches depends on your budget, as even the most exotic creatures, provided that they have enough space, thrive in anything from an old margarine tub kept in the airing cupboard to a more glamorous glass tank set up with all the latest state-of-the-art heating devices.

Since you will at some point want to exhibit your pets to friends and relatives who do not immediately share your enthusiasm, it may be better to keep them in a container that looks good and shows them off to their best whilst at the same time providing them with as near to natural conditions as possible. No matter how hard you try, you will find it difficult to convert someone to your hobby if you have to dig your pet out of a pile of damp, mouldy, rotting fruit and vegetables!

Madagascan Hissing Cockroach on a pile of leaf mould.

Before choosing a home for your pets, first consider the following points.

Escape Proofing

Both cockroaches and millipedes are the greatest escape artists. Cockroaches have flat bodies and easily squeeze into tight gaps. I speak from experience when I say you will be surprised at how small these 'gateways to freedom' can be.

Any vivarium must have a tight-fitting lid that cannot be pushed off. If you use a flat piece of glass or plastic, it is a good idea to weight it down. Millipedes, especially those with a long rounded body and many legs, have evolved their shape to enable them to expend incredible pushing forces, allowing them to plough their way into dense soil and litter to reach food that cannot be utilised by other creatures. This body design also allows them to apply their forces to levering off the lid of your tank.

If you want to breed your animals, remember the young are really tiny and can find their way out of the smallest of holes, so the ventilation holes should be no more than 2–3mm (0.10in) in diameter. A good trick to prevent cockroaches escaping is to smear a 2–3cm (1–1.5in) band of Petroleum jelly around the top of the vivarium, as the insects cannot grip on the slippery surface. Unfortunately, this can look unsightly, attracts dirt and needs reapplying every couple of weeks to remain effective.

Preventing escape is a priority. Not only is it reassuring for other members of your household to know exactly where your pets are located and that they are going to stay there, but it is important for the welfare of the creatures themselves. If they do get loose there is a chance they will not be discovered before they die of starvation, cold or dehydration.

Size

Your vivarium must be capable of maintaining ideal conditions for the animals. Size is probably the first thing to consider. For millipedes, choose something that is at least twice as long and as wide as the length of the longest individual. Cockroaches vary in size but, for the larger and more popular species such as the various hissing cockroaches, a tank of 30 x 15 x 15cm (12 x 6 x 6in) should happily house four or five adult insects.

You must provide a good depth of substrate, such as soil or leaf litter or a mixture of both, about 12cm (5in) for millipedes although cockroaches do not need as much. In fact, cockroaches can tolerate dryer conditions and, as long as moisture is provided, wood shavings or kitchen paper can be used, making them easier to clean out.

Humidity And Ventilation

It is useful to be able to maintain a high humidity. It is critical that a source of moisture is always available. It is especially important with millipedes to keep the substrate damp. Both cockroaches and millipedes have very porous skins: this

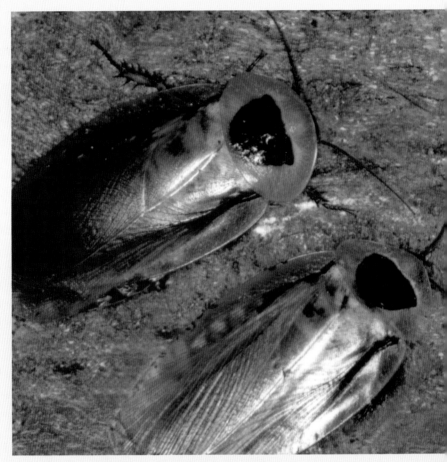

Two adult Blaberus Cockroaches.

means water evaporates from their bodies very quickly. A container with a mostly solid lid is useful to maintain humidity, especially when under-the-tank heat mats are used. The lid helps to keep the heat in and stops the substrate drying out as quickly.

At the same time a degree of ventilation is necessary to stop the air within the vivarium becoming stale and to reduce the conditions where mould develops. Condensation is irritating: it does not affect the animals but it can make viewing difficult. For this reason, it is worth experimenting with the number of ventilation holes in the lid to try to get a balance of all these conditions.

Type Of Container

Glass tanks are preferable, simply because they do not scratch as easily as some of the cheaper plastic versions. They are easier to sterilise with hot water as there are fewer crevices in which potential sources of infection can lurk. The main disadvantages are lack of portability and higher price.

Another commonly available option is the plastic tank, which does have its own advantages. Some have snap-on lids that already have ventilation mesh incorporated into them. Unfortunately for the millipede or cockroach keeper, this provides too much ventilation, so I glue or tape a plastic bag cut to size on the inside. This is a cheap customisation, allowing you to vary the number and position of any ventilation holes you wish to provide.

Old pickle jars are useful for cockroaches, especially young nymphs. Netting tied over the top provides perfect ventilation, but the jars are trickier to clean out.

Heating

Most of the popular pet species available in the world of cockroaches and millipedes are of tropical or sub-tropical origin. Because of this they often need some form of extra heating. Ideally temperatures of between 25°C (77°F) and 30°C (86°F) should be provided. The best way to do this is by using a heat mat. These are fairly cheap to buy and run, and are widely available from most good pet shops. They are often marketed as spider mats or for heating reptile vivariums.

Because different species have different requirements, it is best to create a gradient of temperature within your vivarium. This is easily achieved by placing the mat under one end of the tank, allowing the animals to select their own choice of environment. When setting up a heat mat, be sure to follow the manufacturer's instructions and guide lines.

Heat mats come in a variety of different powers, so before buying make a note of this detail; it can make a great deal of difference. A wattage of 14–16 watts should be sufficient to keep your vivarium up to temperature. At this power it is not necessary to attach the pad to a thermostat although, if you want to be sure you are in control, buy a higher wattage pad and set a thermostat to the desired temperature. Watch that the bottom of the substrate does

Right: A Chocolate millipede.

Hissing Cockroaches. The female is on the left and the male is on the right.

not dry out; check this using your finger. The surface may seem quite moist and you may even have condensation, but the substrate below the surface may be tinder dry, and conditions like this will put the occupants at risk from desiccation.

Alternative ways of heating include running a low wattage (20–25 watt) red light bulb. This is a cheap way of heating from above, although it has the tendency to dry out the surface layers and any condensation that forms can be dangerous. Failing either of the above methods, resort to the airing cupboard. Many species have been successfully bred in the dark, towel-lined confines of the linen cupboard!

Furniture

Vivariums full of soil can look particularly unexciting, especially when the occupants have buried themselves. There are many objects that you can add to improve the visual qualities of your set-up and provide a range of different habitats for the occupants.

Cockroaches in the wild seek intimate crevices in which to hide themselves during the day. They actively seek out areas where both their underside and top surfaces are touching something solid. Tree bark, folded cardboard and egg boxes all work well and what you choose is a matter of personal taste.

Millipedes, on the other hand, have less use for shelter of this kind, preferring to burrow into the soil. This is what they are designed to do, so do not expect your millipedes to be on display all the time. They may well hide out of view for long periods of time, sometimes weeks, without surfacing.

Try adding pieces of bark or small pot plants such as ferns and mosses. They add the interest of a bottle garden to your vivarium as well as helping to maintain humidity and provide extra hiding, egg laying and moulting sites. Plants can be tried with cockroaches but, in my experience, most end up being eaten.

MAINTENANCE

Cockroaches and millipedes have very few needs and are low-maintenance animals.

Feeding

This really could not be simpler. Both cockroaches and millipedes are detritivores which means they will eat just about any dead or decaying plant material.

On the whole, millipedes feed happily on the substrate soil or peat mixed with dead leaves scooped up from the bottom of a hedge or a woodland. Oak is the best, with beech and sycamore coming a close second and third as favourite. This diet can be supplemented with all sorts of other food items and kitchen scraps such as potato peelings, apple cores and tomatoes. It is worth experimenting with a variety of vegetables as each species tends to have its own preferences. Some millipedes have a penchant for meat. This has also been noted in the wild, with millipedes often associated with the carcasses of dead animals. It is worth offering your pet millipedes small pieces of luncheon meat or ham once a week.

Other supplements that provide many extra vitamins are horse and rabbit pellets or even flakes of fish food. Calcium is essential to the growth of millipedes as they need it to form their tough cuticle. A good source of calcium is cuttlefish bone, which can be bought from pet shops.

Female (top) and male (below) African Red Legged Millipedes.

Cockroaches can be fed in a similar way. They do not eat as much soil or dead leaves as the millipedes so give them more fruit, vegetables, leaves, bread and pellets.

It is not usually necessary to supply a separate source of water for your cockroaches unless you are keeping them fairly dry as they can get most of their requirements from their food. It does no harm to moisten them once a day with a mist sprayer (make sure it has never contained pesticides as this will kill your animals) or place a damp pad of cotton wool or moss in an upturned jamjar lid.

Cleaning

Other than regular maintenance, such as removing decomposing food, there is little else that needs to be done. This is certainly one advantage these creatures have over fluffy and feathered pets! Because millipedes do eat a lot of soil and produce copious quantities of dry, round and unscented droppings it is worth replacing the soil substrate in their vivarium about once a month, depending on how much of it they have eaten. To keep any risk of infection low, it is also best to completely sterilise the tank once a year, removing everything, and cleaning the tank with hot water (if it's a glass tank raise the temperature gradually to avoid cracking the glass) and then replacing all the substrate with fresh.

Female Madagascan Hissing Cockroach showing the ootheca.

Female Hissing Cockroach with young.

Unlike many animals that have been kept by man for hundreds of years, owning invertebrates as pets is a relatively new phenomena. As a result, there is still much to be learned about many of these creatures, their behaviour and how many species there are, because more are being discovered all the time.

Choosing A Roach

Despite there being over 4000 described species of cockroach in the world, only about 20 are widely available. Many of these are rather specialised: some are small, some burrow, some are pest species and many of them are very fast runners. These qualities make most of the cockroach world unsuitable for beginners wishing to get to know these beasts. But there are a few larger, slower and flightless species which fit the bill perfectly.

The Madagascan Hissing Cockroach

Approximately four species cultured in captivity answer to this common name and can be quite hard for the beginner to tell apart. However, most live in Africa and the offshore island of Madagascar, inhabit similar habitats and behave in the same sorts of ways. It is the insect called *Gromphadorina portentosa* (grom-far-door-eye-na paw-ten-toe-sa), which is the most widely-available species and one of the easiest to keep.

17

Adult and young Blaberus Cockroach.

Freshly moulted Madagascan Hissing Cockroach.

A female Madagascan Hissing Cockroach in the process of moulting.

Adult Blaberus, showing the wings folded over its back.

This cockroach is a spectacular black and brown wingless insect that originates from the forests of Madagascar. It can grow quite large, about 8–9cm (3–3.5in) long. When alarmed, it squeezes air out of the breathing holes (spiracles) along the sides of its body, making the surprisingly loud hissing sound that gives it its name.

Males can be distinguished from females as often they are bigger, bulkier and have two large bumps on top of the first segment behind the head (pronotum). The males appear to use these in disputes with other males over females, pushing and charging each other with them, and this is often accompanied by a chorus of hissing.

They are probably the best cockroach to keep, primarily due to their size and their longevity. Once adult, they can live for well over two years and are easy to breed. They tend to breed best in groups and you need to have both sexes. You have no idea of what sexes you have until they have moulted their skins five to eight times so it is best to buy large cockroaches that are or are nearly adult; then you can see the bumps of the male if they are present. If you can afford it, a group of four or five is a good starting point.

If at first your cockroaches seem a little skittish, handle them regularly and they will soon become docile and conditioned to being picked up. Soon they will not attempt to run away and, in the end, they will even stop hissing.

If your cockroaches are happy then soon you can expect to see the tiny young, or nymphs, scurrying around. The females do not lay eggs in the way of many insects but produce an egg sac called an *ootheca* (ooh-theek-ah). This is protruded from the tip of the female's abdomen and reabsorbed, and is then incubated inside the body of the female. If you witness this, you will see the long yellow ootheca sticking out of the female's body. Each ootheca can contain 30–40 eggs. The female will eventually give birth to live young, but be careful not to overlook them as at first glance they resemble small, dark woodlice. After emerging they will go through a series of 6–12 skin moults, growing as they go, until they reach adulthood about ten months later.

The Death's Head Cockroach
This is another group of cockroaches from tropical America. They are found in and among rotting wood and are fairly common. They are probably easier to breed than the Hissing Cockroaches, but are best kept by someone who has a little experience simply because they are faster, running for cover at quite a speed. They have a tendency to struggle and this, combined with their speed, makes them unsuitable for a beginner. There are three or four species available and again they are difficult to tell apart and often misnamed.

The most widely available of these insects are *Blaberus craniifer* (blabber-us cran-if-ur) and *Blaberus discoidalis* (blabber-us discoid-are-lis). They are smaller, lighter brown beasts than the Hissing Cockroaches, only growing to about 6–7cm (2.5–3in) in length. Unlike their bigger cousins they have a pair of wings that remain folded like a shield over the back; despite these the insects cannot fly. They get their Latin name, which means 'noxious skull bearer', and their common name of

21

Death's Head Cockroach, from the black blotchy markings found on the adult's back that, with a bit of imagination, look like a skull. The 25–35 young are born live and have a pretty, mottled brown and black speckling. They will go through a series of 9–12 moults and live for about a year as adults.

They can be kept in the same way as the Hissing Cockroaches, the only difference being in the sexing. You have to look at the rear tip on the underside of their bodies. Males have a small, plate-like last segment and the females have a large version of this. There are other differences but these are quite subtle and beyond the scope of this book. These insects go in for a bizarre courtship that appears rather traumatic when seen for the first time. There is a lot of wing flapping and vibrating, and the male raises his wings whilst the female clambers on to his back and begins to feed on secretions produced by glands on his abdomen, prior to mating.

Choosing A Millipede

Even for millipede experts (of which there are few) identifying millipedes is difficult, so do not expect a breeder or a pet shop to know much about what they are selling you, other than it is a millipede! Many are given common names in such instances. African Black or Chocolate Millipede are names that only describe the appearance of the creature and they may be applied to many different species that also fit the description. For these reasons alone it is difficult, if not impossible, to know what you're buying.

Because many millipedes are imported together, the chances are that if they look similar they are the same species, even if you do not know which one! So if you intend to breed, it is a good idea to buy a pair together and not just one now hoping to match it up later with a mate.

Do not worry that you will be over-run with millipedes. In the unlikely event of a huge breeding success, there are plenty of people who will be willing to give them a home. On top of this, not all that much is known about their behaviour so, by breeding them and keeping notes on anything you see, you could well contribute to the greater understanding of these beasts. Some breed more easily than others in captivity so it is worth bearing this in mind when selecting your particular millipede.

The difficulty in obtaining a breeding pair is further complicated in that it is hard to sex them. Males generally have a set of specialised legs on the seventh segment that is modified for mating. These legs are called gonopods and are tucked away in special pouches. An adult male appears to have a set of legs missing. Adult females and immature specimens do not exhibit these. Because it is hard to know how old your millipede is, what may appear to be an adult female could well turn out to be an immature male just one skin moult away from adulthood.

The best practice is to buy as many as you can afford of the same species from the same supplier to increase your chances of getting a pair. Failing this, first identify a male and then look for an individual about the same size or bigger that has not got the gap, and the chances are you have a female.

Everything else is trial and error to get them breeding. Keep them well fed and damp and, if they are going to breed, they will. Generally, millipedes die if they are too cold or too dry. Get this right and they should live for a long time. Most take between four and seven years to mature and live for many more years as an adult. Even the humble Pill Millipede has been recorded as living for 11 years. Very few people have seen millipedes mate, but it is a lengthy process in which the male and female coil around each other and attempt to line up their sexual organs. With all those legs it is not surprising that this can take some time! They lock into an embrace that keeps the front portions of their bodies together, facing each other for several hours. If you witness this, be careful not to disturb them.

The actual egg laying is also quite a secret affair, with the female burying herself into the soil and making her nest. The structure of this varies from species to species but basically it involves laying the eggs in a domed chamber within the soil. Here the eggs are coated with a mixture of special secretions and droppings that protects them from attack by bacteria and moulds. The number of eggs laid in each nest and the number of nests produced varies with the species.

It is hard to specify which species is best when nobody really knows, but here are a few descriptions of common millipede species or animals that fit the same descriptions.

Flat Backed or Plated Millipedes
These belong to the group of millipedes called polydesmids and, as their name suggests, they have a flattened plate-like armour on the top of their bodies. Identifying which species are available is, as with all millipedes, difficult. There are more than 2700 species of polydesmid millipede! I know of a species from Thailand that has recently become available. It doesn't grow as long as other 'snake' millipedes and, having 20 body segments, it only reaches a length of about 6–7cm (2.5–3in), but it is still an attractive creature that is often more active than its larger relatives and, if kept warm and damp, breeds well.

Snake Millipedes
These millipedes belong to the super group called Juliformia. These are the 'Hoover tubes with legs' and they are further split into three groups that superficially all look very similar. They have bodies with a tubular cross section, many legs and often coil themselves up when inactive or disturbed. Many different species come into the country from time to time, most of which are easily bred and cultured. Below is a list of some of the most spectacular and distinctive species but, in most cases, these are probably groups of 'look-alikes' and not separate species.

Red-Legged Millipede
This is a fairly small but very attractive member of the group known as spirobolida. An easy way to identify a member of this order is by a thin line that looks like a join

Thailand Plated Millipede showing its flattened, plate-like armour.

running down the front of the millipede's 'face'. The females, which are often larger than the males, can reach 10–11cm (4–4.5in) in length and have a dull finish to their cuticle (this allows the male a better grip when mating). The males, in contrast, have a high gloss appearance. They are also some of the most colourful of the millipedes, with bright orangey-red legs and head. This species breeds well in captivity.

Zaire Black Millipede
These are large and particularly chunky millipedes reaching lengths of around 16–18cm (6–7in), and they are wider than most. They originate from Africa and stock is regularly imported from the region that gives it the name. They have a very distinctive colour, having a black satin surface to the cuticle. They are easy to keep and breed well in captivity.

Mombassa Train Millipede
This is yet another group of giants from Africa and contains the longest millipedes in the world, some reaching nearly 30cm (12in) in length. These beasts are dark brown, with paler brown rings and are rather slender. Unfortunately, there are numerous giant millipedes that fit this description and belong to the group known as Spirostreptids. It is difficult to be any more precise than this.

Acquiring Your First Millipede Or Cockroach
The best advice is to make sure you buy healthy specimens. This is not as straightforward as buying a guinea pig or gerbil, as millipedes and cockroaches do not really show a lack of condition. Assuming you are able to see the conditions they have been kept in, do not buy if they have come from a dry tank with no apparent source of moisture and be very suspicious if the hygiene levels are poor and there is a quantity of mouldy food lying around. The best test is to see how active they are. Make sure the millipedes are not limp and, if they are coiled up, wait for them to unravel and move. A light sprinkling of water sometimes encourages them. A healthy millipede or cockroach will seem strong, constantly tapping the ground with its antennae and, if gently pulled up from above, the animal should grip tightly. If possible, it is best to buy your millipede from a breeder who should be able to give you information about it. Even if he does not know what type it is, he may be able to tell you something

Left: A species from Uganda that is still unidentified.

WELFARE

about its background, and where it came from. Cockroaches, on the other hand, are easily bred and those you find in pet shops will almost certainly be those species mentioned in this book.

If you keep your millipedes and cockroaches correctly there is little that can go wrong.

Moulting

For each creature this is a very different procedure. The principle is very simple. All Arthropods (animals with a skeleton on the outside of their body and jointed legs), which includes millipedes and cockroaches, have to grow by shedding their skins or skeletons periodically. Cockroaches go through between 6–12 moults as they grow and to do this they simply split their old skin along the back and climb out of it. The insect that emerges is white, soft and crumpled and people who have not witnessed this before often believe that they have a rare species or an albino cockroach. But watch for a few hours and the insect will swell as it expands its body with air to help it to reach its new bigger size, then slowly its skin hardens and darkens to the normal coloration. Do not disturb a cockroach while it is shedding its skin as this often leads to a deformed insect.

Millipedes moult in a similar fashion. At each moult they gain another segment, but they prefer a little more privacy, building a personal changing room from hardened droppings and other secretions which they mould into an igloo-shaped chamber deep in the soil. Safely within this they complete their moult. This is one of the reasons why you should keep disturbance to a minimum and not ferret around too eagerly in the soil, just in case you damage your millipede whilst it is soft and vulnerable. The moulting process in millipedes can take a few days, so do not be alarmed if you have not seen yours for a while. Be patient, and a new, shiny and longer creature will be trundling around before too long.

Health And Disease

If you are unlucky, your millipede may have come straight from the wild and be infected already. If this happens there is little you can do about it. This is another good reason for buying captive-bred creatures and knowing a bit about their history.

All other risks of infections, and pests such as fungi, bacteria, soil mites, moths, beetles and parasites, can be reduced simply by keeping your pets correctly, removing any dead animals, clearing away any festering food and cleaning out the cages regularly. Normally you will not know if an infection is present until many individuals die at once. If this happens, remove any unaffected individuals, completely clean out the vivarium, sterilise it with hot water, and change all the substrate and furniture before returning the animals to their home.

Both cockroaches and millipedes have a tendency to carry small scurrying white or brown mites on their bodies. These appear to do very little harm to the

The feet can be seen clearly on this rolled-up Chocolate Millipede.

animals on which they are living. Most are simply hitching a lift, but if they worry you then they can be gently flicked off with a paint brush and a lot of patience

Things To Think About

Do not put your pets in a situation where they could fall if they release their grip. Millipedes have a habit of doing this and a fall of just 30cm (12in) or so can kill on impact.

Never be tempted to uncoil a millipede forcefully to sex it or try to wake it up. After desiccation this is probably one of the most common forms of death for millipedes in captivity. A good way of coaxing a millipede to uncoil is to spray it with water. Allow it to uncoil in a clear plastic tub, so you can watch for the gap in the legs without having to handle the millipede.

Do not place your vivarium in direct sunlight on a window sill. Despite being tropical invertebrates these creatures do not like light and there is a limit to how much heat they can take. Over-heating will result in them either cooking or becoming fatally dehydrated.

Do not keep millipedes and cockroaches together, as they will often disturb each other when moulting, or eat each others' eggs.

Although cockroaches are fastidiously clean animals it is always a good idea to wash your hands after handling them. It is essential to do this with millipedes. All the millipedes commonly kept in captivity have defensive glands in the form of small pores, normally placed along the sides of their bodies.

These glands secrete a noxious fluid that most predators in the wild find distasteful at the least and deadly in some cases. Fortunately no human has been killed by a millipede. Although the yellowish-brown fluid that leaks from the threatened millipede contains some nasty chemicals such as cyanide, chlorine and iodine, it will do no more harm than stain your skin yellow or black as long as you wash your skin immediately. Leave it and the affected area can become sore and the skin may blister and leave a raw wound, but this can be avoided. Certain millipedes seem to be of a more nervous disposition than others, and are therefore more likely to exude this liquid. However, since so little is known about millipede classification, it is worth treating them all with the same caution.

A selection of 'giant' millipedes.

Zaire Black Millipede.

If you pick up your cockroach, make sure it cannot fall very far.

FURTHER INFORMATION

Organisations And Further Reading

The AES Bug Club
A club for the younger invertebrate enthusiast, with a regular newsletter, livestock, and culture advice. For more details write to: The Bug Club, AES, PO Box 8774, London SW7 5ZZ.

Blattodea Culture Group
For the cockroach enthusiast. Write to Mr Gordon Ramel, c/o IGER, North Wyke, Devon EX20 4SB.

On the Internet: Gordon's Entomological Home Page
http://www.ex.ac.uk/~gjlramel/welcome.html

Gordon, David George (1966), *The Complete Cockroach*.
Ten Speed Press, Berkeley, California. This is a must for anyone besotted with cockroaches, a book full of fun, useful and useless information with which to impress your friends. Essential reading for the beginner.

Hopkin, Stephen P and Read, Helen J (1992), *The Biology of Millipedes*.
Oxford University Press. This is just about the only book available on millipedes which is readable. It is, however, very technical and detailed. It is for those adult enthusiasts who are hungry for information and need to know more, although it is quite expensive.

Once you have had one millipede, you will want to get more.